THE ULTIMATE GUIDE TO MARKETING YOUR BUSINESS WITH

GABRIELA TAYLOR

ISBN-13: 978-1475245967

ISBN-10: 1475245963

Legal Notice

The publisher and author have strived to be as accurate and complete as possible in the creation of this book. The contents within are accurate and up to date at the time of writing however the publisher accepts that due to the rapidly changing nature of the Internet some information may not be fully up to date at the time of reading.

Whilst all attempts have been made to verify information provided in this publication, the Publisher assumes no responsibility for errors, omissions, or contrary interpretation of the subject matter herein. Any perceived slights of specific people or organizations are unintentional.

All Rights Reserved

Dedication

This book is dedicated to my husband for believing in me. Without his unconditional love and support the writing of this book would not have been possible and my life and work would lack focus and direction.

I love you.

TABLE OF CONTENTS

ABOUT THIS BOOK

This book represents over twelve months of research and testing whilst using Pinterest for my clients and my own online presence. I don't believe that any other book currently available about Pinterest will provide you with as comprehensive a guide to the site or as accurate a depiction of the benefits available to both individuals and businesses of using this rapidly expanding media.

How did it all start for me? As an online marketing professional I make it my business to keep up to date with the latest trends and new media. I receive thousands of emails, tweets, posts and blog links everyday and each have their own merits, whether talking about the latest web optimization tools, social networking conferences, technology themes and launches for the year ahead or new social media websites. Usually these trends fade away and I don't hear much else about them however one particular name has been dropping into my world consistently over the past 12 months and has a voice that's getting louder and louder and bigger and bigger like a snowball rolling down a hill...Pinterest.

After hearing so much about Pinterest and it becoming apparent to me that this latest trend was far more than a fad, I decided to check it out. First impressions were not great. As a very organized person my first thought upon seeing Pinterest for the first time was that the site was a complete mess with loads of non-related pictures everywhere on the page. I could not figure out what the site was all about or what it was trying to achieve. However I thought to give it a try and request an invite and the rest is history.

Over the past twelve months I've learned everything I could about Pinterest, use it as much as I would normally use Facebook or Twitter and do find myself slightly addicted to the charms of Pinterest.

Pinterest, once you get to grips with its' quirky ways is an online marketers' dream and I'll explain why throughout this book. This book is a practical toolkit to help you unlock this new social media phenomenon and help you reach your goals whatever they are: build brand awareness, increase traffic to your site, get leads or affiliate marketing sales or simply enjoy the simplicity and beauty of Pinterest.

1
WHAT IS PINTEREST?

Pinterest, the latest social networking phenomenon has exploded onto the scene and has as objective to connect every one in the world through the "things' they love".

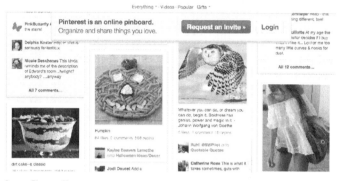

Source: Pinterest Homepage

It has been called a photo sharing site, a shared pinboard, a bookmarking site, a creative outlet, a personalized magazine and many other things. Whatever it is, by October 2012 it had more than 25 million unique visitors (source comScore), with the most usage coming from the UK and US, making it the 4th largest traffic driver worldwide (share of visits: approx. 2%) after Google Organic (share of visits: 40%), Direct Traffic (share of visits: approx. 20%) and

Facebook (share of visits: approx. 6%) (source **Shareaholic**).

January – August 2012 Traffic Sources Breakdown

Pinterest
Yahoo
Bing
Twitter

What it is even more interesting is that the majority of Pinterest users are women, 65% vs. 35% male (AdPlanner). According to a **Pew study** 80% of the U.S. adults are online; 66% are on Facebook, 20% on Linkedin, 16% on Twitter, 12% on Pinterest, 12% on Instagram and 5% on Tumblr.

In the US, fashion and crafts dominate the pinboards, while in the UK Pinterest is mostly used for business purposes and especially for presentations.

Source: Mashable

The Pinterest site (www.pinterest.com) is addictive. Over 20% (2,000,000 members) of the Facebook connected-users are on Pinterest daily. Make no mistake; you will spend hours searching the web, other peoples' boards, and pinning blogs, recipes and articles to your own boards. You will probably also create many more topic boards as you go along. It is not uncommon for people to spend hours "pinning" away.

Some Internet stats actually showed that Pinterest users spend on average 98 minutes a month which is more than the time spent on Twitter, Linkedin and Google+ combined and five times less than on Facebook. And this time spent on the site is one of the reasons for Pinterest being a web marketers' dream. People are on Pinterest for different reasons such as: to pass the time (73%), **to get inspiration on what to buy (70%)**, to collect the things they like (67%) or keep up with the latest trends (67%).

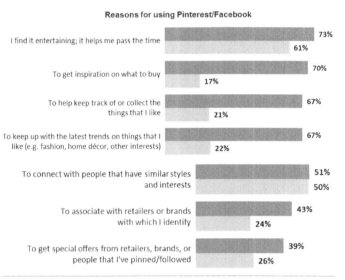

Reasons for using Pinterest/Facebook

	Pinterest	Facebook
I find it entertaining; it helps me pass the time	73%	61%
To get inspiration on what to buy	70%	17%
To help keep track of or collect the things that I like	67%	21%
To keep up with the latest trends on things that I like (e.g. fashion, home décor, other interests)	67%	22%
To connect with people that have similar styles and interests	51%	50%
To associate with retailers or brands with which I identify	43%	24%
To get special offers from retailers, brands, or people that I've pinned/followed	39%	26%

Source: Bizrate® Insights Social Image Sharing and Online Shopping Series 3, August 2012
Q: Do you use Pinterest/Facebook for any of the following reasons?
(n=1,248/4,738 online shoppers who use Pinterest/Facebook)

- Pinterest
- Facebook

Many people may follow you from your other social media sites, but you can also make new friends with similar interests on Pinterest. If you are a foodie, for example, you can find hundreds (at least) of other foodies with which to share recipes. If you love sports or cars, the same thing applies, you will be sharing and pinning in no time.

Pinterest is fun, but it can also be lucrative and it is set to become a vital marketing platform for a wide range of businesses. Writers, Internet marketers, designers, event planners and many others have discovered that Pinterest can draw people to their work or product with little effort. Even for those who are not out to make money, this adventure can be entertaining and educational and is well worth a visit.

2
THE PINTEREST STORY

Different sources show different dates for the start of Pinterest. Wikipedia states that it all started in December 2009 in Palo Alto, California when three friends met to work on a fun project: Ben Silbermann (studied architecture and worked as product specialist at Google), Evan Sharp (worked as product designer at Facebook and founder of HeaderFooter Design) and Paul Sciara (graduated from Yale in 2003 and founder of Cold Brew Labs that was created in 2008 and is now the corporate name of Pinterest).

From left, founders Paul Sciarra, Ben Silbermann, and Evan Sharp. Source: Mathew Scott for Bloomberg, Businessweek

After Pinterest was launched as a beta version in March 2010, it caught on to many more verticals than the founders thought it would. People started to use it to plan birthdays, weddings or vacations, do craft projects, list things they would like to wear or aspired to own and provided tips on many different topics.

Since launch until August 2012 the site has operated on an invitation only basis and this didn't stop the company to grow from 40,000 unique visitors in October 2010 to 3.2 million in October 2011 and then to a remarkable 110+ million unique visitors in May 2012. There are more than 4 million daily unique visitors globally on Pinterest. Please see the graphs below, showing the interest in 'Pinterest' in the last 12 months in different countries provided by Google Trends.

US

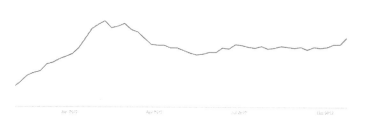

UK

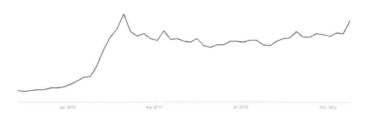

Germany

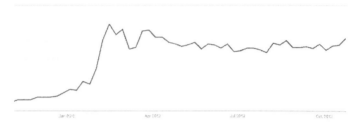

France

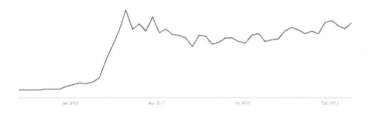

Spain

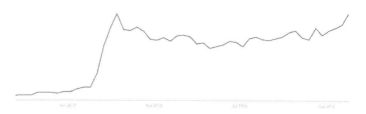

Italy

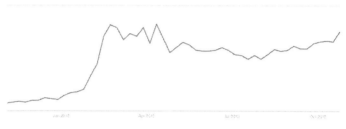

Source: Google Trends

The growth of Pinterest throughout Europe is a phenomenon itself and this, I believe, is only the beginning in terms of adoption, usage and growth.

In Asia Pacific, Pinterest is very popular amongst English speaking countries such as New Zeeland, Australia and Singapore. However the traffic coming from these countries is still very low compared to the traffic Pinterest gets from the leaders in this market. The US alone brings more than 68% of the traffic and the UK in second position brings approx. 3% (see graphic below).

Pinterest's Global Community
Countries and Percentage of Pinterest Users

CANADA 3.3%

UK 2.9%

NETHERLANDS 0.6%

USA 68.6%

FRANCE 1.1%

GERMANY 1.7%

SOUTH KOREA 0.6%

JAPAN 2.4%

MEXICO 0.6%

SPAIN 0.9%

ITALY 2.2%

CHINA 1.5%

BRAZIL 1.0%

INDIA 2.0%

AUSTRALIA 1.6%

SOUTH AFRICA 0.7%

In December 2010, a few months after launch, Pinterest was already listed in the top 10 social networking sites at number 7, ahead of Google+ and Tumblr and behind Facebook, Twitter, Tagged, Linkedin, MySpace and myYearbook (source Hitwise) and was named the best new start up of 2011 (source TechCrunch).

Search Trends shows that Pinterest overtook Google+ in October 2011.

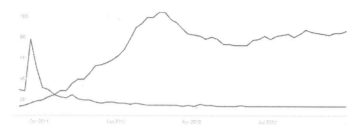

pinterest

google plus

Source: Google Trends

While Pinterest is a more female-friendly platform due to its visual appearance, Google+ appeals more to men and more specifically to students and techies. Women are the most powerful consumer segment and more than 10% of that female segment in Pinterest earns $100,000+ per year. So you can see the potential that Pinterest has for marketers amongst this key demographic.

In April 2012, only two years after launch, Pinterest became the third most visited social platform after Facebook and Twitter. Twitter and Facebook had 3 million (now 182 million+) and 6 million users (now 7 billion+) respectively after 2 years of launch. There are also rumors that Paul Sciarra left the company to join Andreessen Horowitz (one of the Pinterest investors) as entrepreneur-in-residence.

While at Pinterest, Paul was in charge of raising money and other administrative issues. Ben has been focusing on the product and the community and Evan on design.

Besides their website, Pinterest also have iPhone, iPad and Andoid apps and a mobile version of the site.

It is fair to say that the growth of Pinterest has been equally incredible and unexpected. The most unusual thing however about Pinterest is that it has grown so rapidly but so quietly. There is no doubt that Pinterest is much more than just a fad – it will be a big player in the coming years and is around to stay. And whilst it's around to stay, it's around as a web marketing opportunity.

3

HOW DOES PINTEREST MAKE MONEY?

Pinterest, as with many other social networks or user-generated sites in their beginnings, had the objective of not focusing on making money but rather building a product or a platform that users will love and engage with over and over again. It took Twitter and Facebook a couple of years to come up with a monetizing strategy that was not intrusive. Please read below the disclaimer Pinterest put on their site regarding this subject.

"Right now, we are focused on growing Pinterest and making it more valuable. To fund these efforts, we have taken outside investment from entrepreneurs and venture capitalists. We've tested a few different approaches to making money such as affiliate links. We might also try adding advertisements, but we haven't done this yet. Even though making money isn't our top priority right now, it is a long term goal. After all, we want Pinterest to be here to stay!"

The company raised about $37.5 million in 2011 (Yelp, Milo, Bebo, Behance, EventBrite, etc.) and is about to receive another $100 million to fund international expansion from Raukten, the Japanese commerce giant. There is not so much detail about the company's financial situation but it seems that it has an unconfirmed valuation of $1.5 billion (Facebook - $103 billion, Linkedin - $10 billion, Twitter - $8 billion, Instagram - $1 billion) and is probably not making any profit...yet.

Recently, Pinterest experimented with a couple of methods to monetize their site and an affiliate marketing partnership with Skimlinks was one of them. Industry experts say that they've actually done it for about 2 years and dropped it a few weeks ago either after receiving a serious bit of venture capital or when LLSocial.com published an article denouncing their monetizing strategy. Squidoo and Moneysavingexpert also used Skimlinks for a while and then dropped it, as it wasn't making enough money. Just to clarify, Skimlinks is a third party service which automatically identifies links that have an affiliate program and then add an affiliate code to it. Skimlinks usually offers a commission level between 2-5%.

In summary, it is believed that Pinterest has some industry heavyweights behind it in terms of financial clout and investment. It is not believed to be currently actually making any money but that hasn't stopped an unofficial company valuation of around $1.5 Billion. Pinterest is growing at a rapid rate, both in terms of usage and company size, and there are also rumors of other, more established, rivals looking at Pinterest as a possible future acquisition. This is a sign that Pinterest is not only growing in popularity but that it is being taken increasingly seriously as a potential investment opportunity and a major rival to the established elite of social networking.

4

THE PINTEREST CLONES: CAN YOU TELL THE DIFFERENCE?

Whilst Pinterest became popular, many other techies thought to create copycats of it and get a piece of the industry pie. In this chapter I'll provide some examples of sites that look almost identical to Pinterest.

This is not unusual in the world of social networking. After all, if an idea is successful and appeals to the mass market why wouldn't you try to replicate a successful model? This has happened with Facebook, Twitter, Wordpress, YouTube and many more. The common theme however which, in my opinion, I expect to see continue is that copycat sites work, have their place and can be popular. However they will never be as popular or as successful as the original.

RENREN GUANGJIE (j.renren.com)

If you do a search in Baidu, the Chinese search engine you'll find at least 17 Pinterest clones. However the one that presents more interest to us is Renren Guangjie, which translates as "everyone shops". **Renren Guangjie** was developed and launched in January 2012 by Renren (known as the Facebook of China) and mainly links to Taobao, which is the eBay of China.

Source: Renren Guangjie Homepage

GOGOBOT (gogobot.com)

If Pinterest is mostly for creative and crafty people, "Gogobot" is mostly for travel planners. The recommendations you get are coming directly from your social network and are personalized for each one of us. You can also share reviews and photos of the places you've been to or create wish lists. This new social network attracted already major investments from two powerful people in the online industry - Google's Executive Chairman Eric Schmidt and the GM of Square.

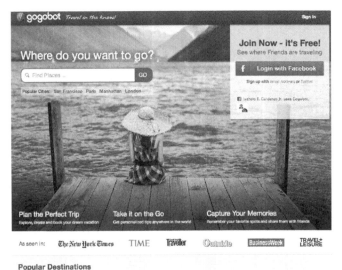

Source: Gogobot Homepage

GENTLEMINT (gentlemint.com)

Gentlemint is another Pinterest clone but this time dedicated to men. It started as a side project that was completed in 12 hours and already has several thousand users and many more on a waiting list. On the Pinterest homepage fashion, make up and nails are predominant. On the Gentlemint you can see pins that feature action movies, cars, whiskey, football, motorbikes, DIY and many more.

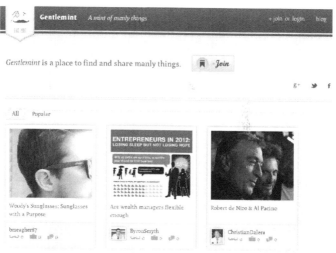

Source: Gentlemint Homepage

PINSPIRE (pinspire.com)

And what about "Pinspire"? Can you tell the difference? It has the same color scheme, the same concept and the same logo. I was shocked when I saw it as the differences are not so obvious. Pinspire was built in Germany by the Samwer brothers who already have the experience of cloning popular sites since 1999 and then selling them. They've done it with Alanda that was sold to eBay, CityDeal to Groupon and Plinga to Zynga.

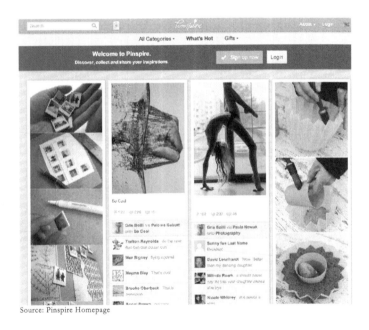

Source: Pinspire Homepage

FAD | IO (fad.io former **mistash.com**)

FAD | IO is a social catalogue of "stashes" or products you already have, want or have previously owned. On Pinterest you can add your own tags or affiliate links, but with FAD | IO there is no way to do this as they automatically add the tags for you.

Source: FAD | IO Homepage

KWAAB (kwaab.com former pintile.com)

Pintile is the Indian version of Pinterest built by Fizzy Softwares that have designed several successful Facebook and iPhone apps. Kwaab.com has recently acquired it.

Source: Kwaab Homepage

PINME (pinme.ru)

We've seen that in China there are at least 17 copycats of Pinterest, but what if we do a search in Yandex, the Russian search engine? Is there any clone? Of course, there is. Pinme.ru is almost indistinguishable and has already attracted some investments (Groupon Russia is one of them). Apart from pinning images, Pinme.ru will also allow product ratings or video downloading.

Source: Pinme.ru Homepage

And the last site (with a very similar interface to Pinterest) I would like to bring to your attention is **CROWD VOICE,** which features videos of protests and news from around the world. There have actually posted a very interesting article about censorship in China that I recommend reading - http://crowdvoice.org/censorship-in-china.

Source: Crowdvoice Homepage

There are many more sites worldwide that copied the Pinterest concept, some of them developed shameless copycats and others niche gems. What makes Pinterest so special and why are so many copycats cropping up? We'll explore this in the next chapter.

5
PINTEREST STANDS OUT IN THE CROWDED SOCIAL MEDIA WORLD

Pinterest is the new next big thing in the world of social networks, at least that's what some experts and businesses believe and it doesn't replace the existing social media tools but offer complementary functionality.

Boticca.com, a jewelry and accessories website, uses Pinterest as an online catalogue for users to browse and then go to the shop to buy. They recently did a test where they compared 50,000 shoppers referred by Pinterest with the same amount of shoppers referred by Facebook. And the conclusion was that users referred by Pinterest spend more money ($180 vs. $85) and less time when browsing the site.

As a referral source, Pinterest brings similar amount of traffic as Twitter and Stumbleupon but much less than Facebook (see graphic below).

January 2012 Referral Traffic
Referral Source and Percentage of Total Referral Traffic

GOOGLE 3.62%
YOUTUBE 1.05%
GOOGLE PLUS
RECENT

FACEBOOK 26.4%

TWITTER 3.61%
LINKEDIN
MYSPACE

STUMBLEUPON 5.07%
PINTEREST 3.6%

Source: www.thesparkleagency.com

In a recent report from HitWise/Experian, both Pinterest and Instagram have been called the "new global stars of social" due to their increase in popularity in several regions of the globe (see table below).

Australia

Instagram: 362% increase

Pinterest: 798% increase

Hong Kong

Instagram: 132% increase

Pinterest: 2,373% increase

New Zealand

Instagram: 843% increase

Pinterest: 643% increase

North America
Instagram: 17,319% increase
Pinterest: 5,124% increase

Singapore
Instagram: 8,121% increase
Pinterest: 623% increase

UK
Instagram: 2,028% increase
Pinterest: 1,489% increase

Other sites that have been very popular are Google+ in Brazil with a 5,750% increase from July 2011 to July 2012 and SkillWho.com with a 7,435% increase during the same period.

Today when the online world is virtually getting flooded with social networks, it is bound to bring up some more newcomers. Some are unique and will last whilst some are unique and fail. Pinterest is definitely going to last.

Twitter was unique and it has reaped the benefits for being different. Facebook was not entirely a new concept back in 2004, but what was new about it was how it went about executing the idea. It takes a great deal of thinking or a quick bolt from the blue idea to hit it big time in the online world.

Below I've listed again **the main players in the social media** industry so you can see where Pinterest currently stands (source **expandedramblings.com**).

Facebook: over 1 billion users worldwide with 600 million accessing the site on their mobile device; more than 42 million pages and 9 million apps

YouTube: more than 800 million unique visitors a month and 4 billion video views daily

Twitter: more than 500 million users and 1.6 billion search queries a day

Qzone: 552 million active users

SinaWeibo: over 400 million users

Renren: over 170 million users

LinkedIn: 175 million members with two new members joining every second

Groupon: 150 million subscribers. 38 million of its subscribers purchased a product or service in 2012 and the average revenue per active user is roughly $70.

Google+: over 400 million members with 100 million of them being active users

Tumblr: 77 million blogs

Pinterest: over 25 million registered users

Pinterest can be safely declared as a social network site or a social scrapbook that is here to stay and is bound to grow. That would not be because of the trend of social networks but because of its uniqueness. Even Facebook's creator, Mark Zuckerberg, recently set up a Pinterest account that already has 10,000 followers. Mark has a new challenge every year: in 2010 he wore a tie every day, in 2011 he was committed to learn Chinese and in 2012 he advised that he will only eat meat from the animals he killed himself.

While **Facebook** had the idea of online friends, catching up with old friends and staying in touch with new ones, **Twitter** had the unique idea of micro messaging and caught the fancy of global celebrities to stay in touch with their fans and followers. **YouTube** created a "sit back and relax as I'll be entertaining you" tool and **Pinterest** has come up with its own unique concept. Pinterest is the social media bridge between emotional and commercial worlds and marketers know that if you can get to one's heart it is much easier to encourage people to buy from you - people buy emotionally and then justify it with logic.

The idea of Pinterest is encapsulated in the term itself. Pinterest has 'pin' and 'interest'. So what one does is pin images that speak of their interest on the pinboard.

It still sticks to the basic aspects of Facebook in terms of liking and sharing content, takes a cue from Twitter as far as the "following" and "retweeting" features are concerned and it is very similar to the "Stumble Upon" model that feeds users ideas from others who have relatively similar "likes". Pinterest also can be loosely connected to Tumblr in the sense that it is also a site which allows users to post blogs that are of interest and users who share the interest can follow such blogs.

Where Pinterest differs is the focus of the social networking site on the idea of sharing images of interest. It is this specialization and no added frills aspect that makes Pinterest truly unique. Not to criticize Facebook or Google+ or Twitter, they are all big names to reckon with and have played significant roles in defining people's online lives, but they have somehow become more of everyone's world without a specific focus. Whilst that works for individuals it does not work wonders for businesses. This is where Pinterest can hit the jackpot. Businesses get an opportunity to actually have a fan following who are specifically interested in the specific domain or topic.

Some of the best and most popular pinboards on Pinterest are those of Fashion products, Lifestyle based pinboards and those that cater to art – painting, craftwork or photography. Pinterest has intentionally kept itself away from doing what the others have mastered and this exclusive feel is what may just give it an edge. Images have more impact than words and Pinterest is a fine example. Most businesses are counting on Pinterest because of the objective centricity of the site. Facebook may be a great way to stay in touch and Twitter may be a fantastic way for a politician or a celebrity to make an announcement but it is Pinterest where one can truly involve a user.

Some companies have already started gaining some serious momentum where users are not only gaining knowledge, but also actively staying posted on several aspects of the business.

Pinterest is geared up to become very informative which Facebook, Google+ or Twitter is not. Sure, they are nice to be on and Twitter does offer an avenue to stay updated about latest stuff from all over the world, but Pinterest is more personalized. You get to discover what you are interested in. It is this interest-centric concept that will work in the favor of Pinterest in the long run. It can act as a solid platform for businesses to meet and interact with true customers.

Social networks need to stay unpredictable, as being mundane would instantly take them off from the top of the charts. Pinterest has left it to the users to keep it in self-discovery mode. It is not based on real time news, a specific product launch or promotion, but instead on exposure to the things that are passions for an individual or business.

Furthermore, through the use of visual bookmarking, Pinterest allows users to show products that they own and love, which in turn naturally promotes those products to other users. This free marketing to the manufacturers of these products has unlimited potential to spread product and brand advocacy.

6

PINTEREST FOR BEGINNERS

Step 1: Setting Up Your Account

There is no need anymore to get an invitation to sign up to Pinterest as in August 2012, after more than two years of service, Pinterest has opened registration up to everybody. And you can also set up both, a personal and a business account or if you have already an account that it is for business you can convert it into a business Pinterest page. Along with these new changes, Pinterest has also published some educational content and case studies featuring businesses that are successful on Pinterest. For more information, click on the link below: http://business.pinterest.com/what-works.

To set up a personal Pinterest account, go to pinterest.com and click on **"Join Pinterest" using Facebook, Twitter or your email address**. It doesn't matter which one you choose to register with, you can link or unlink Facebook and Twitter accounts at a later date.

Create your account to explore Pinterest.

To set up a business Pinterest account, go to business.pinterest.com and **click on either "Convert your existing account"** (if you already have one that needs to be converted into a business account) **or "New to Pinterest? Join as a business"** (if you need to create one for the first time).

We want to help your business get the most out of Pinterest.

Convert your existing account

New to Pinterest? Join as a business.

After that you will basically follow the same steps, except that for existing accounts some of the fields will be pre-filled with information entered previously and also you do not have to follow at least five boards before accessing your account.

So the next step would be to select your "Business Type". Pinterest has provided parenthetical examples for each type to help you.

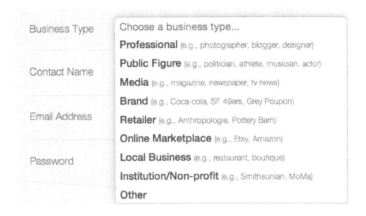

"Contact Name" is not shown publically and you can enter who ever you want. List your company email address in the "Email Address" field.

Your "Business Name" and "Username" should be the same so people can find your brand on Pinterest easily. But not to worry as everything on Pinterest can be reviewed later.

Upload your company logo, write a well optimized description for your business and then enter your website address.

Scroll down to the "Agreement" section and accept it. If this is a new business Pinterest account, you will need to follow 5 boards before being able to access your account. In this way Pinterest will link you with people that have similar interests to your business. If you want, once you set up your account you can unfollow these people.

Now you will need to:
a) verify your website
b) add the "Pin It" bookmarklet to your browser (if you didn't install it yet)
c) add a "Pin It" button to your site to make it easy for people to pin from your site

The verification process is a bit of a challenge for those that are not very technical. My suggestion would be to contact the company that built your site and ask them to do it. The same thing for installing the "Pin It" button to your site; I'm sure they will be able to help with this as well. If somehow you are unable to verify your site, people will still be able to access it by clicking on the little globe, but you will not receive the verification badge, which is a red checkmark, like on the Etsy Pinterest account.

www.etsy.com

To help you **install the "Pin It" bookmarklet into your browser**, Pinterest has created a video that explains how to do it at http://pinterest.com/about/goodies/ and it is browser specific. The bookmarklet will make it easier when pinning pictures to your boards from whichever site you visit with the condition that the site didn't opt-out from Pinterest and has some visual content (pictures, graphics or videos). So drag the "pin it" button to your browser and you are ready to start the fun.

Pin It   ← Add this link to your Bookmarks Bar

To install the "Pin It" button in Safari:

1. Display your Bookmarks by clicking **View > Show Bookmarks Bar**
2. Drag the "Pin It" button to your Bookmarks bar
3. When you are browsing the web, push the "Pin It" button to pin an image

Once installed in your browser, the "Pin It" button lets you grab an image from any website and add it to one of your pinboards. When you pin from a website, we automatically grab the source link so we can credit the original creator.

Step 2: Editing Your Profile

Let's now start editing your profile. To do so, you have two options: either click on "Edit profile" or on "Settings" from the drop down menu at the top right.

BUSINESS TYPE: read the parenthetical examples provided by Pinterest and make sure that you select the closest business type for your business profile.

CONTACT NAME: is not shown publically and you can list who ever you want.

EMAIL: introduce a personal or a business email address depending on your Pinterest strategy. Your email address will not be shown publicly. This is only for communications from Pinterest, including account interaction notifications and the latest Pinterest updates.

PASSWORD: from here you can change your password anytime you want.

LANGUAGES: choose between English, Spanish, French, Portuguese, Dutch and German.

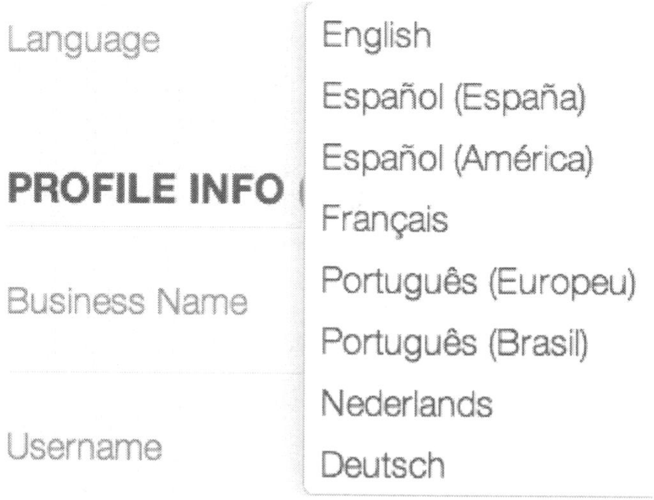

Language

English

Español (España)

Español (América)

PROFILE INFO

Français

Português (Europeu)

Business Name

Português (Brasil)

Nederlands

Username

Deutsch

BUSINESS NAME/USERNAME: use a keyword rich name or your business name.

IMAGE: if this account will be used for business, I suggest you upload your logo or a very good quality picture representing one of your products. You can also use the same image you used for your Facebook or Twitter profile.

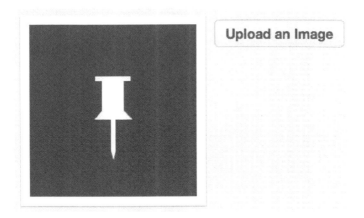

ABOUT: also called "bio" or "profile description". I recommend you mention something about yourself, what your company does, list your products or services in capital letters, explain what your boards will be about and add a call to action. I also advise to feature your website in here and again in the "website" section. There is no limit to the number of characters you use.

LOCATION: for local businesses it is highly recommended that you introduce your full address.

WEBSITE: introduce your website address.

SEARCH PRIVACY: the wording is a bit confusing, so if you want your profile to be indexed by search engines please leave it "OFF".

FACEBOOK & TWITTER: here you can link or unlink your Facebook and Twitter accounts by clicking on "on" and "off".

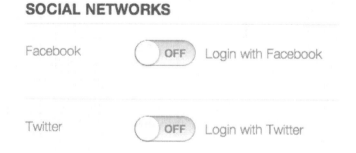

Click on "save profile" and you'll see that underneath your profile description several icons appear: the little globe links to your site (if you didn't verify your site yet), your location and the next two social media icons that link to your Twitter and Facebook accounts (but this only if you entered the login details required in the "Setting" section).

One thing you need to remember is that even if these icons are clickable, for people to access your Facebook and Twitter accounts from your Pinterest account they have to be made public.

Underneath these icons, next to "Boards, Pins, Likes" is a button called "Activity" and it shows your timeline activity in real time and when you or your followers interacted with your Pinterest account. The same information can be seen on the left hand side of your page while you are browsing for pins in different categories.

Step 3: Start Pinning!

ALL ABOUT BOARDS

Before we start looking into "pins and pinning" what they are, how we get them, how they can be edited and so much more, I suggest we start creating some boards.

To access your boards you can either click on "Boards" from the drop down menu or simply on "Boards" just under your profile description.

To create a new board click on the "Add +" button at the top right and then click on "Create a Board".

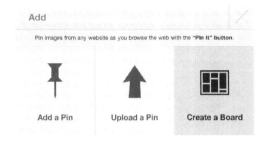

Add a keyword rich board name, choose a category, decide if you want to make it public or private and who can pin to that board.

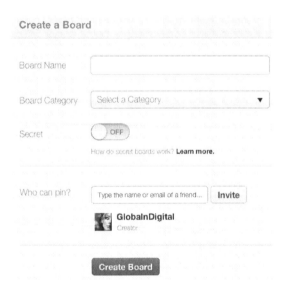

There are 32 (+ Others) categories to choose from and by choosing the right category will help you remain organized and will also allow people to find your pins more easily. However the largest category at the moment on Pinterest is "Others".

1. Animals
2. Architecture
3. Art
4. Cars &Motorcycles
5. Celebrities
6. Design
7. DIY & Crafts
8. Education
9. Film, Music & Books
10. Food & Drink
11. Gardening
12. Geek
13. Hair & Beauty
14. Health & Fitness
15. History
16. Holidays & Events
17. Home Decor
18. Humor
19. Illustrations & Posters
20. Kids
21. Men's Fashion

22. Outdoors

23. Photography

24. Products

25. Quotes

26. Science & Nature

27. Sports

28. Tattoos

29. Technology

29. Travel

31. Wedding

32. Women's Fashion

33. Other

If you do not want anyone to access one of your boards and see the pins within that board, then make it "secret". Only 3 private boards are allowed per person or per brand and they are listed at the bottom of your Pinterest Boards page. This is very useful when you want to collect digital content that inspires you or information on your competitors, but do not want anyone to see it. Also you could create a secret board with membership content (training videos and literature) and only give access (as contributors) to certain people that already paid you for that content. Or you can even have your clients access campaigns reports or details about an event you plan for them.

Another option would be to create a secret board for private photosharing or gift ideas. You can't make a public board "secret" as some Pinterest users may have already repined from that board. However you can make a "Secret Board" public by turning the setting to "OFF" and then people that have selected "Follow All" will automatically follow this newly visible board as well.

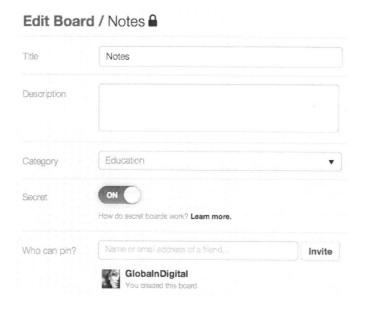

Unless you work on a project that requires input from others such as client collaboration or approval, planning a seminar, a wedding or organizing a vacation trip, I suggest you set the pin authorization to just yourself. If you have several Pinterest accounts and want to feature the same board on all of them, then make yourself as contributor with all your different accounts. So when you update the board, it will do it on all the accounts without the need to log on into a specific account.

To add someone as a contributor, you must follow at least one of their boards. **Group Boards** or **Contributor Boards** are very popular at the moment and it can help increase your follower base or allow your customers to pin images with them using your products. When you see the symbol of a group of people at the top right of a board as in the example below, you know that it has contributors.

If you click on a board that has contributors you can see the contributors at the top left of the page.

If someone follows all your boards and you have a Group Board, then they will follow it as well.

Your boards can always be renamed and rearranged later. To rearrange boards you have to be on your profile page and click the little square located in the middle of the page as in the example below. Always drag the most important boards to the top. When you start with Pinterest it is highly recommended that you create eight boards with 5 pins in each as this is what people will first see when they click through to your profile and empty or incomplete boards don't look great.

To edit the board cover, mouse-over any board, click on "edit board cover" and then choose the pin cover you would like to display and drag it to the position you want. To slice the image cover in several parts as shown below I recommend using the free tool vt.cr/pinterest.

54

To edit a board, click on the "edit" button under the board you want to edit. Here you can change the board title, add a description, decide who will have the authority to add pins to your board, change the category or even delete your board.

Edit a Board

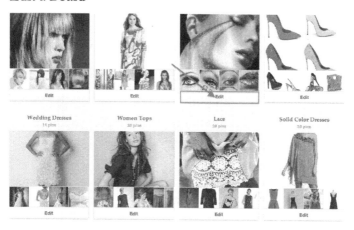

Edit a Board Cover

As we've seen so far, a "board" or a "pinboard" is nothing more than a collection of pins organized by category. So what are "Pins"?

ALL ABOUT PINS

On Pinterest we are all classified according to our preferences. All those pictures, videos, gifts or discussions that we find beautiful or interesting on the web and we tag are called "Pins". Pinterest is often aspirational as people usually collect pictures of something they would like to have or be in the future. However as we have previously explored, people also pin items they own and love. The best time to share on Pinterest is Saturday morning according to Bitly or in the afternoon between 2PM and 4PM EST or between 8PM and 1AM EST.

There are several ways to **find content to pin:**

1) Use the "Pin It" Bookmarklet

While you are surfing the web, and come across something interesting, you can "pin it" to whatever board you like by using the "Pin It" button that you installed earlier in your browser. The pins are actually thumbnails that are linked to the source. The only requirement is that the site you are pinning from has a picture or a video, however no content can be pinned from a Flash site at this stage although this is rumored to be under review and a solution under development.

Let's take an example. Go to Google Images and type the word "flowers".

Choose one of the pictures you like and click on it, then click on the "x" to close the image.

8_flowers+pictures.jpg

This will take you out from Google Images and bring you to the original post that contains that picture.

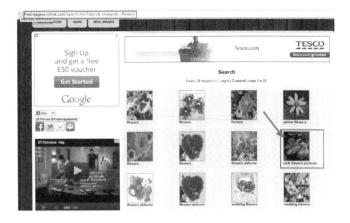

Now click again on the image you want to pin, then click on the "Pin It" button in your browser, mouse-over your pin and then "pin this". Choose the right board for your image or create a new one, add a description and you're done.

600 x 800

Flowers ▼

pink flowers pictures picture , free photo
sharing - via http://bit.ly/epinner

Pin It   422   Twitter

You can also pin directly from Google Images but you need
to make sure that those images are "free to use and share"
(click on the right hand corner and from the settings choose
"usage rights").

This method of pinning directly from the web has created
somewhat of a debate as to whether or not Pinterest
infringes on copyrights. In the US the copyright is unique
and the thumbnail catalogues are considered to be "fair-use"
under United States copyright laws. That said, this is
providing that the owner is cited in the use of their image
and there is still much debate as to whether Pinterest

infringes on copyright laws. It is a US based company, so as long as they act accordingly to US law they are not doing anything wrong. This could be different if it was in non-US territory where the copyright laws are "fair dealing" rather than "fair use". Pinterest clearly states to cite the source of content in their user guidelines. And more recently to defend themselves against copyrighting laws, Pinterest announced that they created a code that can be found in the "help" section of their site that can be added by any site owner at the top of the pages they do not want to share on Pinterest.

So when someone will try to pin the content of that page, they will get the following message: *"This site doesn't allow pinning to Pinterest. Please contact the owner with any questions. Thanks for visiting!"* The Yahoo owned social network, Flickr already took advantage of this new feature and gave its users the option to opt-out from sharing their content on Pinterest by disabling the option to "allow others to share your stuff". However Flickr images with the sharing enabled, have a "Pin It" button and an attribution statement (crediting the author) will automatically be added to all the pictures pinned, below the pin's description. **The difference between a link and an attribution statement** is that the links can be edited and show where the content was discovered while the attribution statements are automatically added, can't be edited and show where the author hosts the content. Attribution statements are also added automatically from pins from YouTube, Vimeo or Behance.

To find the original source of an image found on Pinterest, install the Google Chrome extension "Pin Search" that allows you to perform an image-based search.

2) Browse other people's pins

Another way to find content to pin is to check out other people's pins and "repin" something you like to one of your own boards. Repinning is like retweeting and 80% of the Pinterest users prefer it instead of looking for images on the web or uploading their own. Pinterest has the openness of Twitter as everyone can see your boards and the intimacy of Facebook in terms of the content shared. Creating private boards is not possible at the moment however this is something that Pinterest might implement in the future.

In order to browse other people's pins you have two options:

a)   either you **do a search by keyword** and then browse through "pins", "boards" or "people".

Let's say that I like the dress below and I want to show it on my Fashion board. So how do I do this? I mouse-over the image and then I'm given three options:

- **to repin** it (so get it onto my board without removing it from the original board)

- **to like it** (it gets added to my profile but not to my boards. You choose to "like" a picture if it doesn't fit with any of your board content, but you still find it interesting)

- and **to comment** (this is a good way to engage with other pinners).

In our case we will choose "repin" and in this way we've added a new image to our Fashion board. When you repin, like or comment on someone's pin, they will get an email notification.

b) or you can **click on the "Pinterest" logo** at the top of the page and you'll be brought to a page that shows the most recent pins of other people: from "pinners you follow" to "gifts".

Pinterest

Following · Categories ▾ · Everything · Popular · Gifts ▾

FOLLOWING: it shows all the recent pins from yourself and the people you follow

CATEGORIES: you'll find all the most recent pins in Pinterest sorted by category including videos

EVERYTHING: you'll find all the most recent pins from the 'Other' category

POPULAR: you'll see which pins are the most repinned at the moment and therefore understand the trends

GIFTS: you'll find all those pins that have a price from $1 to $500+ and you can buy gifts by clicking on the picture that has a direct link to the seller

3) Add a pin

And the third method to get pins is by adding them yourself.

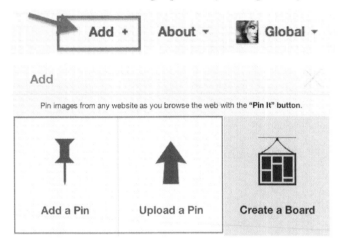

You can either:

a) **add a pin from a webpage** you know the exact url. Only with the website name you'll get a very limited choice of pins to pin.

b)   or **upload an image** that you have on your computer and you have the rights to.

Bear in mind that although the vertical size of the image is not limited, it can't be bigger than 554 pixels in width. Also it is wise to add a watermark with your url and run a search first to see what is the most popular content before uploading yours. If you do not have any great images to upload you can buy stock images and create something new with them.

To create infographics you can use <u>visual.ly</u>. **To watermark your pictures** you can use "<u>Watermark Reloaded</u>", a Wordpress plugin.

We've already seen how we can get content on our boards. Now let's see what else can be done for a successful pinning.

To edit a pin click on one of your boards, mouse-over the pin you want to edit and you'll be given three options: "repin" to one of your other boards, "comment" or "edit".

Versus . Spring 2012. Absolutely amazing!

tumblr.com

Edit Pin

Description — Versus . Spring 2012. Absolutely amazing!

Link — http://www.tumblr.com/dashboard

Board — Skirts

Delete — **Delete Pin**

Save Pin

In the description you can add a keyword rich description or just keywords separated by a comma, introduce your affiliate or website url and choose the right board to put the pin in. As we've seen so far, pins are organized in pinboards and each pinboard is part of a category. Pinboards can be re-arranged easily, however it is not so easy to do this with individual pins. At the time of writing Pinterest is looking into this.

Mentions in Pinterest

If you want to recommend or notify a user about a pin you have to follow at least one of his boards and introduce the symbol "@" (at) followed by the username of the person either in the pin's description or in the pin's comment.

Hashtags in Pinterest

You are probably aware of the symbol "#" (hashtag) in Twitter that are attached to a keyword to make it easily searchable. In Pinterest you have to add this in the picture description and you can't use it more than three times when you describe one pin.

Commenting on a pin

As I mentioned earlier, the best way to engage with another user is by commenting on their pins. However if you change your mind and want to delete your comment you can do it by clicking the "x" on the right side of the comment. By following the same process you are also able to delete other users comments on your pins.

Adding a price to a pin is very easy. Anywhere in the pin's description you can type the dollar ($) or the pound (£) symbol followed by the amount that has to be higher that 1. At the moment it doesn't work with any other currencies, however the Euro (€) should be implemented soon as it is

Pinterest's third biggest market and one that we know is growing rapidly.

Video Pins

Pinterest is mostly known for sharing pictures, however since August 2011 people can also share videos. To add videos to your boards from YouTube or Vimeo, you can either "add a pin from a webpage you know the url" or use the "Pin It" bookmarklet. To find the correct url of a video you want to share from YouTube, find a video you like and then click "share" underneath the video. Copy the url on the left and then paste it onto Pinterest.

Get your pins to go viral

The top 10 sources for pins are:

Source: Zoomsphere

Pins can go viral in a matter of seconds and be seen by millions worldwide. Funny quotes, recipes, cute kids or animals, infographics, contests and videos seem to be amongst the most popular in Pinterest and have the potential to go viral. This global and viral potential is again a web marketers' dream and has so much commercial potential when promoting a product.

Step 4: Getting Followed

You can either get people to "follow all" of your boards, which basically means following your profile or "follow" individual boards. The same way you follow you can at any time unfollow users or boards and users will not be notified about this.

Follow a profile or all boards

Etsy
Everywhere
Follow

Follow a specific board

In order to see who is following your profile or who you are following on Pinterest you need to go to your profile and then click on "followers" or "following" at the right as shown below.

In order to see how many people follow one of your boards click on the board and at the top right you'll be able to see the number of followers for that board and the number of pins "curated" so far. Unfortunately at this moment it is not possible to see details of your board followers.

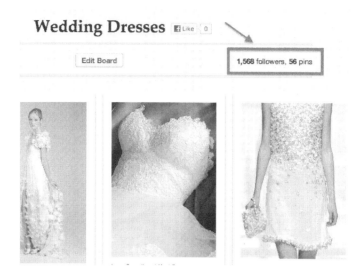

Wedding Dresses Like 0

Edit Board

1,568 followers, 56 pins

To increase your number of followers you need to:

- Post all of the time: upload original content, repin other people's pins or use the "pin it" bookmarklet

- Find people in your niche and follow them; hopefully they will follow you back. To find people in your niche you can check the followers of the ones you already follow and follow them, do a search by keyword or check the "everything" category and look for your niche

- Follow back people that follow you and also follow their followers

- Interact with people who have a big number of followers, comment on their stuff, like it or repin it

- Install the "follow us" and "pin it" buttons on your site

- Add a "follow us on Pinterest" link to your business signature in emails

- Make a "How I use Pinterest" video on YouTube with a link to your profile and, in turn, pin your videos from YouTube

- Mention other users in your comments or pin descriptions to get attention

- Post valuable "comments" on pins featuring on the Pinterest homepage or the "popular" category. This will help you gain visibility for your account and attract more followers. All your comments will have a backlink to your profile and people may follow you

- Post viral pins: beautiful, educational, inspirational, useful or funny

- If you have a list of customers, invite them to join Pinterest and to follow your profile. You can either invite someone by entering their email address or by accessing your Facebook, Gmail or Yahoo contacts. Blocking users that you do not want to follow you is not yet possible but is being considered by Pinterest.

To block users that you do not want to follow you or interact with your pins go to their profile and click on the flag on the right-hand side of their profile description. For more details on this topic you can click on the link below:

https://support.pinterest.com/entries/22153837-how-do-i-block-someone

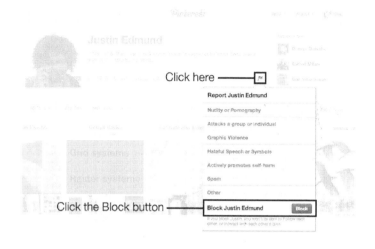

Step 5: Take The Visual Conversation Outside Pinterest

If you like a pin and want to share it with others, Pinterest gives you several options: to like it, to tweet it, to embed it in a webpage or to email it to someone who would be interested to know more about it. However if you find a pin that you consider "offensive", you can report it to Pinterest and they will remove it immediately.

YouTube and Pinterest

• make a video showing how you use Pinterest for your business and post it on YouTube with a link to your Pinterest account

• use the call-to-action overlay on your own videos and link to your Pinterest account

• pin your own videos

To show your most recent pins on your site on the sidebar I suggest you install the Wordpress plugin "Pretty Pinterest Pins". You can choose whether to show the description below the image and the number of pins to show. You can also feature the latest pins from any user.

Sharing to Facebook

If you haven't yet updated to Facebook Timeline you will not be able to share your pins. However when you pin or repin make sure that you tick the checkbox for sharing and links to your pins or boards will be shared on your status updates. Bear in mind that people do not want to be notified every time you have a new pin on your boards, unless it's a useful one to them.

If you like all the pins from a specific board you can click "like" at the top of your board and it will be shared with your Facebook friends.

You can also display all your Pinterest boards or pins on Facebook by installing an app called "Woobox" or show your Facebook posts in a similar fashion to Pinterest by installing an app called Pinvolve. Another option for cross-promotion would be to promote your Pinterest contests on Facebook.

Sharing to Twitter

If your Pinterest account links to your Twitter account you can share your pins every time you pin or repin by ticking the checkbox for sharing.

7
HOW TO CASH IN WITH PINTEREST?

At the time of updating this book, October 2012, Pinterest is ranked #38 globally by Alexa (#15 in the US), had a Google page rank of 7 and a SeoMoz domain authority of 96/100, 765k total links, almost 2.5 million fans on their Facebook page, 1 million followers on their Twitter account, 12k Google+1 and more than 23 million users. The time and opportunity to learn quickly and benefit from Pinterest is now, as it readies itself for global explosion. If you figure out how to use Pinterest for business purposes before any one else, you can become a leader in your industry.

Pinterest is fast becoming one of the best, if not THE best marketing tool of any of the social networks. For a rather new social network, the pinboards are easy to share and fun to read without taking up too much of your time.

For products or services, Pinterest can take your business to a whole different level. All it takes is a few "Pin It" and your business can easily take off. So before you engage in asking for an invitation, be sure you're ready for new traffic and orders.

The best part of Pinterest is that it doesn't matter what type of business you're in. For example, a website called Child's Own Studio, who make soft toys from children's drawings, was doing fine with 4 to 5 orders per week. Someone "Pinned" this site and now the owner has so many orders she can't keep up with them. She also receives over a hundred emails a day. And this with a website that is not even hosted on an owned domain and has no online payment facilities.

— by Oliver McDougall, age 5

Source: childsown.wordpress.com

According to a survey organized by PriceGrabber where 5000 people were interviewed, 21% of the respondents advised that they bought a product after seeing an image on Pinterest. The most commonly purchased products were food related, fashion, home decorating and crafts.

So, you can see where Pinterest will be key to your marketing strategy and the remarkable traffic it can bring. Here are few industries that can benefit from using Pinterest.com. Bear in mind that Pinterest can't be automated yet and an actual person needs to be involved.

Freelancers – any type of freelancer such as a photographer, writer, web designer or other can double or triple site traffic when utilizing Pinterest in marketing plans. One "Pin It" can bring in more work than you can handle. Showcase your products or services in a visual and catchy way, add a description and link back to your site. That's all you have to do or as Joel Comm said in one of his books "Like me, Know me, trust me, pay me!". You can also create an ebook or any other incentive and offer it as freebie to increase your list.

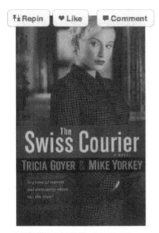

The Swiss Courier. Free for Today
(Feb. 1) only! $0.00
Christianbook.com, Amazon.com ...
spread the word!

Nicole M. via Tricia Goyer onto
BookPile

Retailers – you can't actually sell products through Pinterest
but you can let the people know you have a product they
may like and you can also list the price. When you post your
product, usually as an image or video, pinners will repin it
and share it with their friends on Facebook and Twitter, not
to mention all their followers on Pinterest. You can also link
back to your website, create exclusive bundle offers, run
promotions, offer coupons or even collect testimonials from
people wearing or using your products. In order to sell
better you have to create desire and inspire people.

Remember: good marketers know that they do not market products, but a lifestyle!

Travel agents – if you're in travel you can pin travel destinations, hotels, cities, restaurants, places to visit, and things to see in any spot in the world. You would create a special board to showcase your destinations with images of the city, things to do, places to eat, and even recipes will get you a response from pinners. The beauty of Pinterest is that you attract attention and interest from the images of your destination products and can then link back to, and drive traffic to, your main website.

Source: tumblr.com

Home decorators – Some pinners are using Pinterest to build their dream house. They gain insight into designs from all over the world. They look for tips on how best to layout their house, what type of lighting, floors, and kitchens and some of them will end up buying the product. If that happens to be your company, you just yourself got a customer with not too much effort!

moroccan home of fashion designer Liza Bruce

elledecor.com

Pink + orange.

sayyestohoboken.com

Real estate agents – list the best real estate images you have and link back to your site

Luxury Villa in Dubai

1220 South Ocean Boulevard, Palm Beach, FL $74,000,000

Beauticians, Personal shoppers or wedding planners - the top three pin topics in Pinterest at the moment are actually related to beauty: nails, eyes and hairstyle. As someone in charge of the image of your clients you could suggest specific looks and update on the current trends.

Restaurant owners – can share ideas for recipes, cocktails, new menus and even interiors.

Affiliate marketers – an affiliate marketer can increase traffic to any product they recommend. The boards are loaded with wish lists from people looking for the best products for their homes, backyards, and gardens and complete outfits to wear for casual wear or for a night out on the town.

They repin, and their friends repin, and so on... you do not even need a website! Just decide on your niche and start pinning. And with each pin you can use straight affiliate links from Amazon, eBay, Clickbank or CPA Offers (Peerfly). Cosmetic surgery companies pay up to $40-$50 for a qualified lead. Why not work with them to provide some new customers? I also advise to test different pictures, videos, formats or layouts and post them at different times of the day or days of the week to see which work better. There is no set format or formula for Pinterest. Trial and error can often produce the best, and most surprising, results. **And remember 80% of the pins are repinned while only 1.4% of tweets are retweeted.**

Project owners – as a group of people working on the same project, Pinterest gives you the option to add contributors to your board. And you can also do market research or collect feedback on a product in development.

Teachers or coaches – if you have something to teach, Pinterest is a great resource to upload lessons plans, video tutorials or motivational quotes. And students can post back if you allow them to contribute to one of your boards.

PR specialists – Pinterest is great for branding. You can display your client's logo, web pages, offices, employees, case studies, launch a daily pin theme, provide news, etc.

SEO strategists – take advantage of link-building opportunities and use of keywords. Until recently all the links from Pinterest used to be "dofollow", but there are still some ways you can get some dofollow links and I'll show you how in the advanced strategies chapter. You can also use Pinterest for local SEO or video marketing.

Pick an industry and Pinterest can be one of the best marketing tools in your arsenal. However, you do need to use it the right way. It's not like the whiners on Facebook, or the Tweeters who let you know what they do throughout the day. If you want a response from the rest of the pinners, then you have to pin the way it was set up to pin. That's what they want on Pinterest, something that will help them, inspire them, lift their mood, give them a reason for living, and other ideas to make their life better. If you can supply that without hard selling to them, they will repin you often. Repining is how your message goes viral.

No matter what industry you're in or whether your business is large or local, there are undoubted marketing opportunities to be had from Pinterest. Whilst there is no magic formula in the over-populated world of online marketing, Pinterest can really help to drive traffic to your site. And, as we know in online marketing, traffic means money.

8
LEARN FROM THE MASTERS

The Most Pinteractive And Engaging Brands

It was not until a few months back that Pinterest managed to attract any attention. Despite being around for almost two years, the social photo-sharing site remained significantly distant from a larger audience or in actual fact it was the other way around. Anyway, some companies have been a step ahead on Pinterest and have been steadily gaining more prominence on the site, growing their followers count and are also managing to engage the users. Here are 10 brands on Pinterest that have actually managed to do the right things in the game.

Mashable

Mashable, the techno news site, is one of those very few brands on Pinterest that is thinking ahead of its time. Pinterest has been a bit of a ladies' favorite till now and and Mashable's content is not much of a favorite with the traditional female consumer. Mashable however has understood the significance of having a presence and understands that men will inevitably hop on to the Pinterest bandwagon. Mashable could end up way ahead of the other techno sites that sign up hurriedly to Pinterest in the future without a proper strategy.

nothing but good.

CHOBANI®

GREEK YOGURT

http://pinterest.com/chobani

6,256 followers

760 following

22 boards

1,426 pins

154 likes

Social marketing is not about what you actually do but how you engage your audience. Chobani seems to have mastered this art. Despite their domain being that of Greek yogurt, they consistently share some interesting info about food items, different recipes and some unknown facts. They have been steadily growing their base of followers and are definitely one of those brands that have taken up the right strategy on Pinterest.

http://pinterest.com/birchbox
20,000 followers
787 following
23 boards
2,683 pins
184 likes

When a site has about 60 to 70% female users, anything that has to do with beauty and fashion would certainly be one of the most favorite hotspots. Birchbox manages to pin various contents on beauty, fashion tips and several products as well, which keeps the female followers glued to their updates. Birchbox has shown that Pinterest is not simply about sharing some pictures but that one can innovate. Birchbox uploads videos about their products and a plethora of information. They are perhaps one of the best companies on Pinterest who have been employing some very successful promotional strategies. Birchbox also has a Pinterest account dedicated to men called Birchbox Man that has about 300 followers and more than 700 pins.

http://pinterest.com/wholefoods

72,000 followers

1,150 following

45 boards

1,119 pins

17 likes

When a brand has a vision and a philosophy then it must do something to promote that ethos to a wider audience. Whole Foods is one of those rare brands that may not be trying to have an impact on sales but they intend to promote their motto. The retail brand manages to put up content very regularly about good food and rude food, hygiene and other updates on green living.

▮ SCHOLASTIC

Books need to be promoted as much as movies and music. Scholastic does exactly that by uploading several images of book covers and promoting existing and upcoming books and updates on publishing. They also have some interestingly funny aspects to their pinboard such as people dressed up as book characters, drawing a lot of attention to the brand.

http://pinterest.com/bhg

205,000 followers

90 following

96 boards

3,500 pins

252 likes

We are always interested in ideas for our homes and gardening tips. Any brand that is associated with contents on lifestyle and decorating ideas would immediately catch the fancy of users on Pinterest. This is exactly what the brand Better Homes and Gardens have done with their profile.

Where Creativity Happens™

http://pinterest.com/michaelsstores

85,000 followers

7,000 following

57 boards

2,600 pins

630 likes

The concept of Pinterest initially was to pin pictures and share what one would like. Michaels Stores is perhaps one of those brands that naturally falls into this category on Pinterest since they deal with craftworks and anything to do with creativity is sure to have sufficient resonance on Pinterest. Their efforts of sharing new ideas and creating projects are good ways to maintain interest and an active pinboard.

Etsy

Any eCommerce site must be on Pinterest and Etsy was one of the earliest to cash in on the trend. It is not only one of the rare brands to have a massive following but is also high on activity. Etsy does not only try to sell their products online but instead shares a lot of innovative ideas to make one's own goods and how simple stuff can be made and used by users at home.

http://pinterest.com/generalelectric

12,000 followers

512 following

21 boards

1,394 pins

338 likes

General Electric uses Pinterest to share their products, history and lineage and also have a dedicated space for their fans to have a presence on their profile. The brand allows users and fans to post creative contents that would be of interest and be inspiring to others.

www.peapod.com

Online grocery shopping & delivery

http://pinterest.com/peapoddelivers

1,800 followers

45 following

65 boards

1,700 pins

30 likes

We know things can be delivered to our doorstep, be it groceries or a laptop. Peapod allows users to take a sneak peek at the inside workings of running a delivery system and lets you discover their world, a unique way to promote your business.

Who Are The Power Pinners?

Pinterest is a fantastic web site for sharing what you love. The site creates such a powerful world of digital organization that some people can feel overwhelmed by what they find there. In this chapter I will show you the top power pinners who've made the most of Pinterest so you can visit their profiles and pinboards and find out what has made them so great.

Melissa Alonzo-Dillard

http://pinterest.com/mel_dillard
14,583 followers
3,500 following
124 boards
10,157 pins
296 likes

This woman knows what she loves and her area of expertize is one which is a great resource to many. She has more than 80 boards dedicated to teaching and teaching skills. If you are a teacher starting out on Pinterest she blazes a trail that few others can follow. There are many other teachers on

Pinterest who share the love of their craft but Melissa is ahead of them all on creative and resourcefulness. Her avid interest in her own field and her expert use of Pinterest to display it shows her dedication and her clear ability. It is people like Melissa that make Pinterest such a wonderful site. They take their real world experience, knowledge and interests and turn them into boards for people to enjoy and learn from. Her profile is full of boards that will help you learn much more about teaching. For any education professional Melissa's profile is one to follow.

Keegan Adriance

http://pinterest.com/keegsandkels
4,500 followers
152 following
53 boards
2,883 pins
0 likes

If photography and design are your thing then look no further than Keegan Adriance's profile for inspiration and ideas. She has almost three thousand pins and over five hundred thousand followers all because of her creativity and her willingness to share it. Her boards include accessories and clothing for men and women. She also fills up her profile with her own work in photography and design and shares her favorites in the field with everybody. Keegan's quality boards are always worth looking at and you may go back to them again and again. They are full of inspiration for everyday life, something we all badly need sometimes. Her position on this list stems from her absolute interest in everything she does. Whether it's food or drink, dogs, tilt shift photographs or pictures of her ideal camera equipment she brings a passion to her pinning. This is why her boards are so popular and why she is an established power pinner.

Marine Loiseau

Marine's Pinterest boards are simple and elegant. All of her interests on the site stem from one thing, beauty. She takes the everyday occurrences we take for granted and points out the beauty in them, finding such everyday beauty distilled in

104

a photograph is incredible. Her unique way of looking at the world has earned almost a quarter of a million followers and over three hundred likes. If you're bogged down in life or stuck in a rut rummage through her boards. Her excellent "skin... light" is full spectacular images of light interacting with the skin, and is one of my personal favorites. Her ability to take a simple concept and elevate to art is an incredible testimony to her unique vision. She is the best at what she does and for that deserves a place as a power pinner in this list.

Ben Silbermann

http://pinterest.com/8en
808,507 followers
70 boards
3,768 pins

It's no surprise that Ben is a power pinner, he's the CEO of Pinterest itself. He knows exactly how to use the site and it shows. He has almost one hundred boards active and thousands of pins. When Pinterest started in Beta in March 2010 his was one of the first profiles on there. He had a head start in the pinning world but that's not the only thing that makes him great at it. He has boards from all over the spectrum. He shows all of his interests and sometimes simply puts up something funny, entertaining or heartwarming to let you relax and enjoy your pinning experience. Ben's profile even has many boards specifically for men, who happen to be only a small percentage of Pinterest's users. If you need inspiration look to Ben's boards. He knows what he's doing, he founded the site, and he is certainly a power pinner.

Note: Ben recently closed his account and started a new one where he has about 5,000 followers. He wanted to experience how new Pinterest users would feel.

Jane Wang

http://pinterest.com/janew
6,700,000 followers
193 following
95 boards
20,000 pins
2,300 likes

Ben's mum is also someone to learn from. She is actually the most followed pinner by far. The next most followed pinner has only half of the followers that Jane Wang has. Jane managed to build almost 100 boards all from a broad range of interests such as "issues", "octopus", "guy", "fun with kids" or "DIY alternatives to the infinite".

If you have looked at these amazing pinners (brands and individuals) you must now have a better understanding of the right way to approach Pinterest. The important factor is that all of the above share their interest for what they do and their sincere wish to share their love. If you have the same attitude you will have no problem excelling once you get the hang of it and one day you may even become a power pinner yourself!

9
ADVANCED PINTEREST STRATEGIES

The world players in search at the moment are Google for text search, YouTube/Google for video search, Pinterest for image search and Visual.ly that recently announced their aim to become the leader in infographics search.

Now that we've learned the basics of Pinterest and seen some of the masters in pinning, I would like to guide you in this chapter through more advanced strategies such as Pinterest SEO or how to track and measure results in Pinterest.

Pinterest SEO

We've seen so far how great Pinterest could be for your business, but are you ready for Pinterest? A good optimization of your website, your Pinterest profile, pins and boards can help you get found, pinned, repinned and followed and therefore increase traffic to your site.

1. IS YOUR SITE OPTIMIZED FOR PINNING?

In order for your site to be optimized for Pinterest it is highly recommended that:

a)   you use permalinks (URLs to your individual weblog posts. Last part of the url after .com or any other extension used, should contain your keyword)

b)   all your posts have a visually appealing image

c)   all your pictures have alt tags and watermarks with your url

d)   you have installed the "follow me" and the "pin it" buttons. Both buttons will take people to your Pinterest profile where they can choose if they want to follow one of your boards or all of them

To install the "Follow me" button onto your Wordpress site:

1.   Select the type of button you'd like to appear on your site

2. Copy the code provided on the right side of the button

3. Go to Dashboard > Appearance > Widgets > Available Widgets

4. Place a text sidebar widget wherever you'd like your button to appear

5. Paste in the code

6. Replace "username" with your Pinterest username and save

To install the "Pin It" button underneath your posts on your Wordpress site:

The easiest way to have complete control over what gets pinned from your site is by installing the <u>Pinterest "Pin It" Button</u> plugin that has already been downloaded 20,000 times. With this plugin you can choose where you want your "Pin It" button to appear: above or below the posts, on your home page, individual posts, static pages and archives.

2.   OPTIMIZE YOU PINTEREST PROFILE

To optimize your Pinterest profile, make sure you link to your site and your Facebook and Twitter accounts and also include your keywords in the "first or last name" and in the "about" section on Pinterest. For your username I would suggest that you add your business name. For local SEO (Search Engine Optimization) it is recommended that you include your city in as many sections as you can. You can also add your full address and contact details.

In order to be indexed by search engines do not forget to leave the visibility in your profile to "off". Your first and last name will be the ones that appear as a title in search engines.

Until recently all the links in Pinterest including the one to your website from your profile were "do follow" links. Now the only "do follow" links you can get are the ones from the url of a pin and the url that you included in the pin's description, however they can be replaced easily when an image is repinned.

One last tip I have for better optimization of your Pinterest profile is to submit your RSS feed url to RSS Feed Directories. To find a list of the most popular RSS Directories, just do a search in Google but I would recommend using www.pingler.com, which really helps with this. You can either ping your profile or just a board.

User feed: feed://pinterest.com/username/feed.rss

Board Feed: feed://pinterest.com/username/board/rss

3. OPTIMIZE YOUR PINTEREST BOARDS AND PINS

Optimizing your boards: make sure you add a keyword rich description of up to 500 characters for each one of your boards without falling into keyword stuffing. Also choosing the right category for each board will help users find your boards more easily. When the category is not added to a board, Pinterest will ask your board visitors to select one for you and you may not want this. The title of your boards has to be short, interesting and include your keywords.

Optimizing your pins: as with the boards, pins also have their own description and it is highly recommended that you include your keywords here separated by a comma and the source url. Also do not forget to also the add the url in the pin's link section. When adding a description to a pin you can use:

• **hashtags ("#")** in front of your keywords so your pin can be easily found. Don't use more than three in one description

• **mentions ("@")** in front of the username of one of the pinners you are following to engage with him/her

• **"likes"** for other people's pins if they are interesting but do not match your topics

It seems that Pinterest ranks pins in the search results by the keywords in the description, the number of pins, comments and likes.

Tracking and Measuring Results

When an image is pinned from the web it automatically gets the source URL. If you feature visual content on your site it is possible that some of it has been already pinned and you are getting traffic from Pinterest.

To check if your site has been already pinned and if your URL was correctly added type the following link on Google by replacing "yourdomain.com" with your site domain: pinterest.com/source/**yourdomain.com.** If you find any of your images and you are not happy with the way they've been tagged, you can always email the user and ask him to make the corrections required.

Once you start uploading your own pins, I advise that you constantly check pin stats and which are the most popular so you know which kind of content you should share on Pinterest. To check stats on a pin, click on the image as in the example below and underneath you can see how many times it was repinned, liked or how many comments it has received.

There is also a very useful tool on the Internet that helps you **measure your popularity and influence on Pinterest**. To sign up to Pinpuff (pinpuff.com) simply enter your email address and username. You get stats such as scores for your account, reach, activity or virality as well the number of followers and following, likes and liked, pins and boards, repins, etc. To spy on your competitors you need their username and then type the following url in Google by replacing "username" with your competitor Pinterest username: http://pinpuff.com/user/username

We've seen earlier some of the power pinners as brands and individuals. If you are looking for people to follow you can start with them and also check a tool called Zoomsphere (http://www.zoomsphere.com) that shows **the most influential people or brands on Pinterest**, Facebook, Twitter, Google+, YouTube or Linkedin. You can access it freely and it is updated weekly.

Most followed people on Pinterest

Source: Zoomsphere

Most followed brands on Pinterest

Source: Zoomsphere

To track traffic and sales to your site I recommend Google Analytics. As each pin has its own URL, I suggest you check the referral traffic. You can also set up goals and give them a value.

10
30 TOOLS TO ENHANCE YOUR PINTEREST EXPERIENCE

While Pinterest has been able to grow their user base in a very short period of time, several companies have noticed the phenomenal growth and interest for Pinterest and came up with associated **apps and supporting tools to enhance your Pinterest experience**. This is nothing new since we had seen similar developments with Twitter, Facebook or YouTube.

ONLINE TOOLS

1. ZoomSphere (zoomsphere.com)

With ZoomSphere, a user can get popular updates and trends from Pinterest and other social networking sites (Facebook, Twitter, YouTube, Google+ and Linkedin). You can see the brands and the profiles with the most followers as well as global stats and which Pinterest accounts have the biggest number of pins and likes. All this information is provided for free, however for more detailed charts there is a monthly fee of $99.

2. Pinerly (pinerly.com)

Pinerly is a user-friendly dashboard that allows clear control and management of your Pinterest account. Using this tool, you can easily measure and optimize your pins to Pinterest. Start by creating 'campaign pins' from a web link or a pin you uploaded from your computer. The tool allows you to add cool effects to the image you pinned via their site and also provides stats such as clicks, likes, repins and reach. More than one Pinterest account can be tracked at the same time. It is not yet open to the public so you can join by using the following link: http://www.pinerly.com/i/a6l1Z. And in order to be able to access all their features you need to invite 5 other people. New features will be added soon such as getting paid for "spreading the word" (for publishers) and promoting your content (for advertisers).

3. Repinly (repinly.com)

Repinly provides insights (see graphs below) into what is trending on Pinterest in different categories and also helps finding the influencers in your industry so you can follow and learn from them.

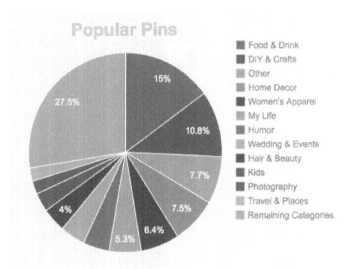

Popular Pins

- Food & Drink
- DiY & Crafts
- Other
- Home Decor
- Women's Apparel
- My Life
- Humor
- Wedding & Events
- Hair & Beauty
- Kids
- Photography
- Travel & Places
- Remaining Categories

15%
10.8%
7.7%
7.5%
6.4%
5.3%
4%
27.5%

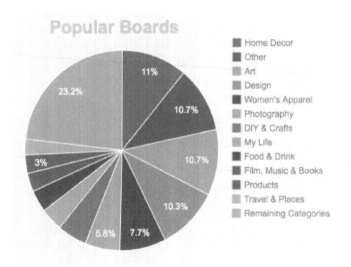

Popular Boards

- Home Decor
- Other
- Art
- Design
- Women's Apparel
- Photography
- DIY & Crafts
- My Life
- Food & Drink
- Film, Music & Books
- Products
- Travel & Places
- Remaining Categories

11%
10.7%
10.7%
10.3%
7.7%
5.8%
3%
23.2%

Average Activity of Popular Pinners

 2472 Pins

 32 boards

 following **331**

How Users Spend Their Time on Pinterest

86.2%   13.3%   0.5%

Pinning   Liking   Commenting

4. Pinfluencer (pinfluencer.com)

Pinfluencer is predominantly an analytics tool. The primary objective of Pinfluencer is to offer data such as top pins, top viral boards, top influential pinners, influence and engagement scores and it compares your Pinterest activity (new pins, new repins, pins/day, new followers) to the activity of your top competitors. The tool is free to try for 60 days.

Besides this, a new feature was launched in October 2012 called "Pinterest Promotions" (pinfluencer.com/promotions) that allows brans to organize contests and sweepstakes ("Best PinBoard", "Win By repining from the brand's board", "Win by pinning website content", etc.) on a Facebook tab/own website and then convert Facebook fans or customers into brand promoters on Pinterest.

Jonathan Goldmann, Head of Social at Jetsetter.com advised, "With Pinfluencer we were able to easily run a successful scavenger type contest recently and saw a 2,400% increase in Pins/Day, generating close to 4,000 pins and repins that reached over 7 million Pinterest users. Pinfluencer's Promotions dashboard, with its Omniture,

Coremetrics, and Google Analytics integration, tracked not just participants and pins, but also ROI metrics like revenue and clicks and made the reporting very intuitive."

Below you can find Pinterest screenshots (featuring contests and sweeps winners) from Gilt, eBay and Sephora that already took advance of the Pinfluencer new feature for promotions.

Pin to Win:
Gilt Wedding Style!

Create a bridal pinboard inspired by this **Carolina Herrera** applique gown for a chance to win a **$2,500** Gilt shopping spree, plus **$2,500** towards a honeymoon on Jetsetter.

Click for details.

GILT

eBay via eBay

Repinned 11 days ago from **Dorm Livin'**

Congratulations @April Smith for winning the Dorm Room Sweepstakes! Your prize is on the way!

 Add a comment.

Pinned onto the board

Sweeps Winners!

Follow

Originally from **Dorm Livin'** by

eBay

Follow

Pinned via **pinmarklet** from

rover.ebay.com

3 Likes

SEPHORA PRESENTS

PAINT THE TOWN
—— S W E E P S T A K E S ——

REPIN TO WIN!
Get your nails set for the holidays and enter for your chance to win
one of ten **SEPHORA BY OPI TINSEL TOWN COLLECTOR'S SETS!**

HOW TO ENTER
1. Follow us at **Pinterest.com/Sephora**

2. Repin any image from our **SEPHORA SWEEPSTAKES board**
and include **#SephoraSweeps** in the pin description.

3. Go to **http://sweeps.pinfluencer.com/sephora** and enter
your Pinterest username & email by **October 26**.

5. <u>PinPuff</u> (pinpuff.com)

PinPuff is another tool to gauge trends and it measures an

account's popularity among the users of Pinterest and the

value of each pin. By entering your email address and

Pinterest username you will find out your Reach Score, Activity Score and Virality Score. A Pinfluence score above 50 is a good score and brands would love to include you in their Pinterest strategy. PinPuff also gives a monetary value to the pins and traffic you generate. Recently a new feature called "Perks" has been added and it allows pinners to earn gifts based on their influence.

6. ShareAsImage (shareasimage.com)

Although Pinterest is primarily about images, quotes and content cannot be ruled out. With ShareAsImage (previously called "PinAQuote") you can highlight and pin text from any web source onto Pinterest. To make it easier they even created a "ShareAsImage" bookmarklet that you can drag to your Bookmarks Toolbar very much like the "Pin It" button. It can also be used to share the same content at the same time to multiple other social networking sites. By paying the one-time fee of $6.99 you are allowed to personalize your image quotes by adding special effects and colors.

7. SpinPicks (spinpick.com)

This photo spinning app was initially named "Spinterest" and now after some revamps they have come up with their new brand name, "SpinPicks". The app allows users to log in with their Pinterest account or an independent account and spin creative common images from different visual platforms such as Pinterest, Instagram, Twitpic, Flickr, Reddit, YouTube and PicPlz. The only ones excluded from this list are Google.com, Facebook.com, Tumblr and Bing and this to avoid copyrighting issues. There are also other features such as pinning or liking a pinboard or even following a specific user but this would require the user to be logged in to Pinterest. However I would say that the best feature is the "auto-spin" where one can pick a category and the visual platform from where they would like to look for content and then click on "click to spin". A few seconds later SpinPicks will suggest some awesome content that you can then repin to your Pinterest board.

8. PinGraphy (pingraphy.com)

This is a great tool that allows you to upload pins in bulk (from a website or your computer) and schedule them to show on Pinterest at the time you want.

9. WiseStamp (wisestamp.com)

WideStamp is possibly one of the best tools to use with Pinterest as it transforms an email signature into a promotional tool by adding the "Follow Me On …" button (any big social network including Pinterest) at the bottom of one's signature in emails. You would need to download this tool and get it customized with your email signature and links to your social media accounts and you are then set. For Pinteresters, WiseStamp has a surprise. Once you have created your signature and pinned it to your pinterest board with the tag "@WiseStamp" in the description, WiseStamp will repin it to their "Your Signature Here!" board. Do not forget to add your link to the pin signature.

10. Visual.ly

Visual.ly is a tool that allows people to create graphical content using the data they have and without any software or in depth knowledge about animation or any graphics whatsoever. Pinterest, being a site for images and hence graphical content is a perfect partner for Visual.ly. It is a one of a kind tool that would come in handy for almost every user that has an account on Pinterest. As Visual.ly has currently the biggest infographics database, it can also be used as a source for your pins.

11. Pingler (pingler.com)

Pingler is a free tool that allows users to ping a URL to multiple websites, blogs and forums or onto social networking sites. Using Pingler, one can easily enter the website or webpage name, upload the website URL and decide the category where it should be pinged or posted. They have a free subscription as well as a premium one, albeit with extra features and facilities.

12. vt.cr/pinterest

It can be used to slice, resize or crop your images before uploading them onto Pinterest.

13. PicMonkey.com

PicMonkey allows easy editing of pictures and creation of collages. Several options for image personalization are available such as: variety of fonts, textures, backgrounds, shadows and frames.

14. PinWords (pinwords.com)

This is a great tool that allows users to add beautiful text to their images. You can upload an image from your computer, enter the URL of an image from the web or use one of their backgrounds. There are 6 themes for the images and 8 types of fonts.

See below examples of images edited with PinWords.

You affect the world by what you browse (Tim Berners-Lee)

You affect the world by what you browse (Tim Berners-Lee)

IS THIS SUPER AWESOME THEME

WIDE

ENOUGH FOR YOU?

15. <u>Pinstamatic</u> (pinstamatic.com)

This is my favorite tool. It is free and you can do so much with it. No registration is required.

a) **Website**: enter a website address and take a screenshot of the full page and post it directly to Pinterest (similar to Snapito or URL2Pin).

b) **Text**: choose a background (pink, plain, grunge, impact, colors or chalk – see examples below), introduce a quote and its author and then pin it to Pinterest.

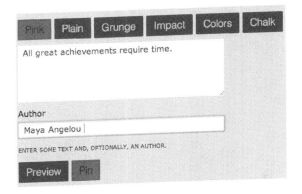

All great achievements require time.

Author

Maya Angelou

ENTER SOME TEXT AND, OPTIONALLY, AN AUTHOR.

Preview   Pin

All great achievements require time.

~ Maya Angelou

All great
achievements require
time.

Maya Angelou

All great
achievements
require time.

- Maya Angelou

ALL GREAT ACH..

~maya angelou

ALL GREAT ACHIE...

~ maya angelou

All great achievements
require time.

- Maya Angelou

c) **Sticky**: create yellow sticky posts with your quote

d) **Spotify**: share your favorite tracks to Pinterest. If pinners have Spotify account when clicking on your pin they will be able to play the song in full.

e) **Twitter**: create a visual representation of a Twitter account.

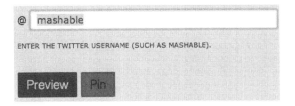

f) **Date**: add a date to a Pinterest board to show to let your followers about an upcoming event.

g) **Place**: share a place of interest

h) **Photo**: add bottom and top captions to your photos

16. Pinvolve (pinvolve.co)

It helps bridging your Facebook and Pinterest presence, which means that your updates on Facebook will be displayed just like you were on Pinterest. You must be logged into your Facebook account to be able to install the Pinvolve app. See example below of a Facebook page that has the Pinvolve app installed.

Each post will have two buttons (a "Pin It" and a "Share" to Facebook button – see example below) allowing you more interaction with your fans/customers.

Pin it   Share ➔

Here is the 3rd and final Parents' Wisdom question. It's slightly different to the usual but Lisa Barnwell Pregnancy & Early Postnatal Care is wondering if you agree or have any further 'bugbears' to add to this list.

0 likes   0 comments

 MamaBabyBliss onto Here is the 3rd and final Parents' Wisdom question. It's slightly different to the usual but Lisa...

17. WooBox (woobox.com/pinterest)

WooBox is a Facebook app that allows the display of Pinterest boards and pins as a tab on your Facebook Page.

18. PinAlerts (pinalerts.com)

It lets you know if someone pinned something from your sitxe and who pinned it. Once you discover who shared your content a good thing to do is to thank the sharers and follow them on Pinterest.

19. PicMarkr (picmarkr.com)

With PicMarkr you can add custom watermark (picture or text) to your pictures before uploading them on social media sites.

GOOGLE CHROME EXTENSIONS

It is perhaps expected that when a social networking site or any online avenue goes viral, popular web browsers would bring in tools and extensions for easy maneuvering of content posting. Google Chrome is not one to miss out on such aspects and here are some of the extensions that are already available for free.

20. Pinzy

Pinzy is a cool app to have. Once you have this extension in place, you do not need to click on an image on Pinterest to have a larger view, nor is there any need to open it in another window or tab. You can simply hover on the top of the image and the larger size of the image would appear at the same resolution quality and without altering the page.

21. Screen 2 Pin

This is again a tool to post a screenshot from anywhere on the web directly to Pinterest. The difference with the others tools is that you do not need to enter a URL or take a screenshot using the keyboard button. You can simply click on the toolbar icon which will automatically capture the URL you are on and you can post it directly. The same extension tool on Google Chrome can also be used to post screenshots to Twitter and Facebook.

22. Pin Search

Pin Search is certainly one of the most interesting app for Pinterest. For a long time the predominant way of searching the web has been through text search. This app is really unique as it now allows us to search by an image. We can use Pin Search to search a picture and grab all the information associated with the image: sites where the image is featured, similar pictures and other details such as the designer or the photographer who created it.

23. Pinterest Pin It Button (by Shareaholic)

While there are several "Pinterest Pin It Buttons" available online, the one by Shareaholic also allows the user to learn the number of times a specific pin has been repinned. That is certainly a new feature which many people would like to take advantage of.

24. Extended Share for Google Plus

This Google Chrome's extension allows users to add a "Share on…" link to each Google Plus post. And you can add as many as 19 social networks links: Pinterest, Facebook, Twitter, Linkedin, Tumblr, StumbleUpon, etc.

25. 99Pixts

This Chrome extension works with Pinterest, Facebook, Twitter and Tumblr and allows insertion of smart text into your photos.

WORDPRESS PLUG-INS

WordPress is certainly one of the most widely used tools to post content online and there is no surprise that Pinterest plugins have been created.

26. Pinterest Pin It Button

It allows adding the "Pin It" button to your WordPress site or posts so the readers know that they can easily pin your visual content onto their Pinterest boards.

27. Pretty Pinterest Pins

With the "Pretty Pinterest Pins" widget you can easily create a customized and neat sidebar where you can post all the latest pins on Pinterest or pins from specific pinboards (yours or from other users). This is a convenient way of highlighting some content that you would want and also the quality of your profile at one glance. Having a "Follow me on Pinterest" button at the bottom of the Pretty Pinterest Pins is also a great idea.

28. NextScripts

This is a plugin that automatically posts your blog content to several social media networks such as Pinterest, Twitter, Facebook, Linkedin, Google+, Tumblr, StumbleUpon, etc.

29. Watermark Reloaded

There were already a few copyright issues with Pinterest in its early days and whenever images and videos are concerned, there is bound to be copyright violations.

Watermark Reloaded is a simple tool to put your signature as a watermark on the images that you own. This is perhaps the easiest way to ensure that your images are safe and cannot be misused or widely distributed without an acknowledgement of your ownership.

30. Pinterest Block

If you do not want your pages or posts to be pinned on Pinterest, use this plugin. All you have to do is to add the meta tag *<meta name="pinterest" content="nopin" />* to the content that you do not want to be pinned.

11
WHERE TO NOW?

That's just few of the things you can do on Pinterest as a business. Now it is time to start pinning. Pinterest is taking off now and the opportunity is immediate. There are many web strategists who say it might take over Facebook. I won't comment on this possibility as Facebook has itself been a phenomenon however I would point out that Pinterest has grown at a rapid rate and has already out "trafficked" many other social networking sites. It's growing and it's growing fast. If you do it right, it can be a better marketing tool than Facebook, Google+, and Twitter put together not only because of its growth rate and potential but because of it's unique approach.

So far, Pinterest has proven it can help to significantly improve traffic to your website, increase sales, but also run contests, do marketing research, and brand your name to millions of pinners. What more can you ask for from a marketing tool?

In summary, I would like to list all the keys steps I've outlined in this book that will help to turn your experience into a successful pinning.

Step 1: decide if the Pinterest account is for personal or business use.

Step 2: define your Pinterest goal: drive traffic to your site, get leads, increase sales, build brand awareness, do market research, test new product concepts or even educate.

Step 3: know your target market. Any company can do well on Pinterest with a bit of creativity. Different generations, cultures and gender have a different approach online.

Step 4: define success metrics – what results do you need to get to consider yourself successful on Pinterest.

Step 5: set up your account.

Step 6: install the "Pin It" bookmarklet into your browser.

Step 7: optimize your site for Pinterest.

Step 8: optimize your Pinterest profile.

Step 9: define a content strategy and create interesting and well optimized boards. Be creative with your boards and keep the titles short. Get personal: create a board that tells the story of your company in a visual way. No empty boards. Put the most popular boards at the top. Have at least 8 boards with 5 pins each. When you get new better pins remove the weakest ones. Optimize your boards with the right keywords.

Step 10: start pinning! Pin your own blog, website or Youtube videos. Pin other people's stuff. Pin everyday (at least 30 minutes a day) and lots. Add prices to your pins if you sell products.

Step 11: optimize your pins. Add proper captions, edit your links, add call to action, include prices if appropriate, use videos and create original content. With powerful pins you can relax as once they go viral others will do the work for you.

Step 12: build credibility and expertise through your pins: *teach* (video tutorials and infographics), *share results* (before and after), *tell your story* and add value.

Step 13: engage with your audience: repin, comment, like, mention, cross promote with other social networks. Find influential pinners and follow them. Invite your contacts (Facebook, Tweeter, YouTube, Linkedin, Gmail, etc.) to join Pinterest and follow their profiles.

Step 14: be creative with your boards and pins. They are like a page on your site; surveys in the form of a picture and people can comment underneath, contests for the best testimonials or slogan, coupons, QR codes with a surprise message, guest pinner boards, pins of the week, exclusive product bundle, invitation to an event, product focus group where people can vote with likes, links to freebies to build your list, etc.

Step 15: track and measure results. You do not want to do things without knowing if it brings any value. Use all the **Pinterest Goodies** and make use of the tools recommended in this book.

Thank you for buying my book. I hope you enjoyed it and found it extremely useful as a current or potential Pinterest user, whether that be consumer, commercial or as an online marketing professional. I write my books with tremendous passion, only to make sure readers like you enjoy it to the fullest. Now that you've finished reading this book, I am kindly asking you to write an honest review on Amazon, even if you did not like it. Your constructive feedback will help me improve my books, and your positive feedback will help other Amazonians choose if they want to buy my book or not. To write your review, please click on one of THE LINKS below:

US: http://www.amazon.com/dp/B007J3HFWM

UK: http://www.amazon.co.uk/dp/B007J3HFWM

IT: http://www.amazon.it/dp/B007J3HFWM

ES: http://www.amazon.es/dp/B007J3HFWM

FR: http://www.amazon.fr/dp/B007J3HFWM

This book is constantly being updated and edited to add new resources and remove the ones that have faded away. Therefore, the book you have downloaded today may in fact have newer updates. If you'd like to be notified when changes are made please send me an email to info@globalndigital.com, so I know that you are interested in receiving updated copies of this book as soon as they are released.

Happy And Successful Pinning!

ABOUT THE AUTHOR

Gabriela Taylor is an internationally educated Global Online Marketing Strategist and Consultant who's worked with some of the world's biggest brands in Telecommunications, Retail, Lifestyle and Advertising.

A recognized expert and specialist in Social Networking, Mobile Marketing and Search Engine Optimization she is fluent in 7 languages, has lived and worked in many countries throughout the world and has experience of implementing successful web-presence strategies for both startup and large established organizations.

She is the founder of Global & Digital, a consultancy firm specializing in Online Marketing services and Cross-Cultural business practices and has also published several industry related books.

ALSO BY GABRIELA TAYLOR:

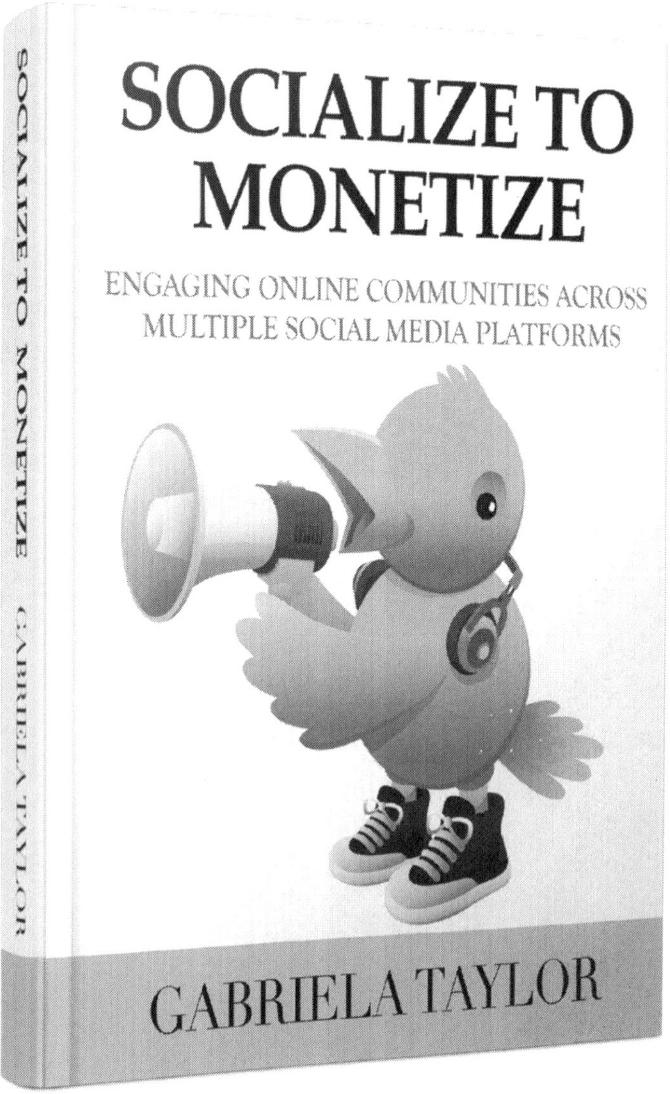

SOCIALIZE TO MONETIZE
ENGAGING ONLINE COMMUNITIES ACROSS MULTIPLE SOCIAL MEDIA PLATFORMS
GABRIELA TAYLOR
SOCIALIZE TO MONETIZE GABRIELA TAYLOR

Utilizing Social Media networks to launch, grow and maximize any business or online marketing strategy is absolutely essential in this digitally connected and dependent world. The opportunity to reach a wider community and customer base, grow your network and to stay abreast of social media trends is key to driving success. This can also however be a confusing world where new networks and fads are literally springing up daily. It can be tempting to join an overwhelming number of social media sites without any real idea of how to make the most of your online presence. While most of these platforms are valuable to your brand, it is essential that you know how and when to use them effectively for maximum return.

Throughout this book I will cover some of the most important social networks and how to use them to your advantage and grow your business. You will also learn how to build and engage a community across multiple social media platforms and build the right marketing strategy and campaigns that create social buzz and brand awareness.

The Ultimate Guide To Building And Marketing Your Business With ...

Google

A Step By Step Guide To Unlocking The Power Of Google Tools And Maximizing Your Online Potential

GABRIELA TAYLOR

Google is an intrinsic part of our daily online lives. It is the world's largest and busiest search engine by an immeasurable margin, is widely used for online email storage, as a map and navigation tool, is a rapidly growing social networking site and is the number one choice of the masses when searching for images and video content.

There is no doubt that we have a massive reliance on Google for our entire online experience. There is also no question that Google is a incredibly successful organization that has transformed our online world, made huge amounts of money through it's successful advertising strategy and is absolutely essential for any business that wants to make money online. Just how can you though, as a small business, make the most of the vast array of tools that Google has to offer?

This book unlocks the power of Google and how you can make this search giant work for you and your business. Learn more about the full suite of Google Tools (YouTube, AdWords, Google SEO, Google+, AdSense, News, Analytics, etc.) and how you can use them to launch & grow your business.

ALSO BY GABRIELA TAYLOR:

The Internet literally offers thousands of free solutions that will support your marketing and advertising campaign. Some, naturally, are better than others and some may appear to be free at first but have hidden costs attributed to them if you want to use them for effective commercial purposes. There are however many fantastic free tools out there that I have tried and tested and it is definitely possible to build and market your business for ZERO COST using these tools.

Why pay for online tools when there are fantastic free ones available that will massively benefit your business and that cost you absolutely nothing? This book will take you through some of the best tools available, will provide you with the top tips you need to succeed and will also give you a host of useful links to online resources.

The most remarkable aspect of taking your business online is that it is accessible by everyone and anyone across the globe. However, just because it is possible for businesses to reach people in different countries does not mean that all the potential customers in these countries will be receptive to the message that you are relaying. As such, when you take your business global, it is important that you optimize your website to accommodate the anticipated barriers and logistics of dealing with diverse countries and international requirements.

From the cultural differences and considerations of dealing with different regions to key tips for growing your online business, this book is the perfect companion for any marketer or business owner looking to maximize their global online presence and reach.

ALSO BY GABRIELA TAYLOR:

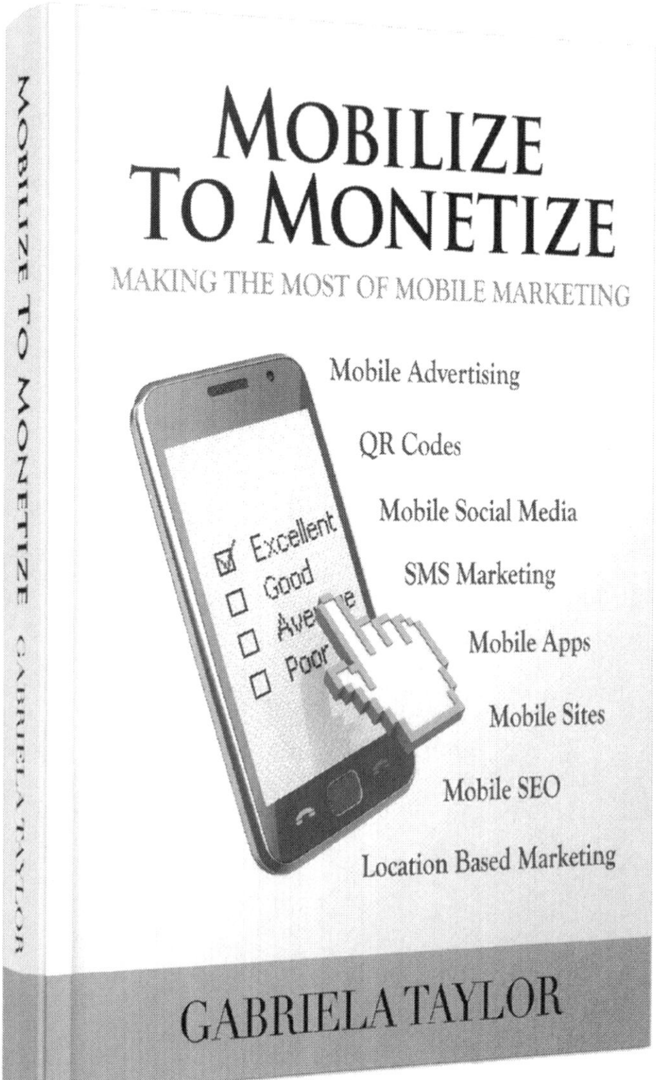
MOBILIZE TO MONETIZE
MAKING THE MOST OF MOBILE MARKETING
Mobile Advertising
QR Codes
Mobile Social Media
SMS Marketing
Mobile Apps
Mobile Sites
Mobile SEO
Location Based Marketing
Excellent
Good
Poor
GABRIELA TAYLOR
MOBILIZE TO MONETIZE GABRIELA TAYLOR

The advent of the Internet as a tool that can be used to enhance business processes and its ability to function on any device including mobile phones has unveiled limitless marketing possibilities. Most mobile users already consider mobile devices as important personal assets. Consumers continue to rely on these devices more and more throughout the day and for different purposes. As such, mobile users are more likely to pay attention to messages and marketing information sent to their mobile devices.

Throughout this book I will cover the advantages and disadvantages of mobile marketing as well as 12 ways of engaging with your mobile community. Mobile marketing, when used effectively, can be the holy grail of marketing allowing you to target and contact your customers on the go.

Online advertising has brought with it more benefits than traditional marketers could have anticipated. With online advertising and marketing you can reach more people at a global level, you can target your messages to be more relevant to your audience, you can interact with your community and collect their feedback in real-time, you will need a smaller budget and you can monitor results and make changes on the go.

Throughout this book, I will cover some of the most common forms of online advertising and also provide tips on how to better improve your online advertising experience as a business owner or marketer.

ALSO BY GABRIELA TAYLOR:

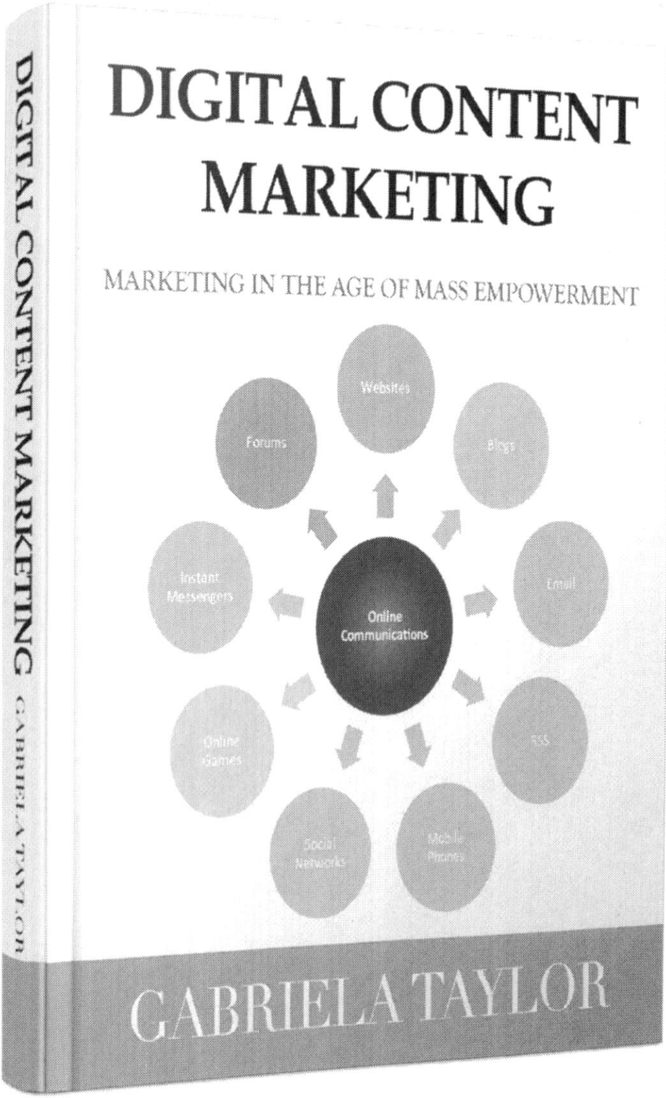

DIGITAL CONTENT MARKETING

MARKETING IN THE AGE OF MASS EMPOWERMENT

Websites

Forums

Blogs

Instant
Messengers

Online
Communications

Email

Online
Games

RSS

Social
Networks

Mobile
Phones

GABRIELA TAYLOR

Engagement marketing is a move from one-way campaigns to a strategy that seeks to have dialogue with the customer. Unlike traditional forms of marketing that bombard and interrupt the customer, engagement marketing leverages the specific needs of the customer. It is also about encouraging customers to interact among themselves, which can build advocacy for your brand.

Throughout this book I will cover some of the best strategies in content marketing including areas such as content planning, content creation, content optimization, and content distribution. You'll also learn the different types of content, the pros and cons of free and paid content or the difference between content creation and content curation. That's just few of the things you will learn from this book that will conclude with a section on content performance measurement that will show you the diverse metrics and tools that you can use to determine how well you are achieving your content market goals.

ALSO BY GABRIELA TAYLOR:

Get Your Copy Now

The world is changing. The way we do business, the way we shop, the way we socialize and the way we run successful marketing campaigns. Tumblr, as a tool for business, will help you take your marketing strategy to the next level. If pictures are worth a thousand words, Tumblr is worth its weight in gold.

Throughout this book I will take you through some of the key features of Tumblr as both an intermediate user and an expert lookg for advanced strategies for making Tumblr work for your brand. I will show you how Tumblr can be utilized as a fantastic tool to showcase your brand to a worldwide audience and will then also go one step further and demonstrate the power of creating a social buzz. I will provide you with some great ways in which you can cash in with Tumblr and also suggest some of the best tools and resources out there to use in conjunction with Tumblr.

ALSO BY GABRIELA TAYLOR:

Demographics play a huge part in today's marketing strategies. Understanding your target market and how to target marketing campaigns to different generations, genders and cultures allows the professional marketer to maximize their success and demonstrate true commerciality and return on investment.

Throughout this book, Gabriela Taylor discusses socio-demographic profiling and covers the key traits of a wide array of potential customers. The author also looks at the social networking phenomenon and includes some of the key profile types on Facebook, Twitter and Klout. Social Media Networks are the first platforms that provide a clear direction on the likes and dislikes of certain groups or individuals and the author brings to life how such insights help to better understand an individual's life cycle, interests and purchasing habits.

A comprehensive guide to targeted demographic marketing, this book will help any marketer understand their audience better and help them to target the right market for them in the right way.

19358208R00095

Made in the USA
Lexington, KY
15 December 2012